Bespoke:
The Handbuilt Bicycle

Lars Müller Publishers

New York, a city of pedestrians and taxis, is also a city of bicycles. Each year, countless riders don helmets and pedal to school, work, and cultural attractions for exercise or the simple thrill of the ride. A growing culture of cycling is taking shape across the city, most visibly through the creation of bike paths down the length of Broadway, starting at the door of the Museum of Arts and Design on Columbus Circle.

This rise in the popularity of cycling has been accompanied by an increasing fascination with bicycle design and construction. Extraordinary examples can be found in the pages of this publication: custom-fitted, handbuilt metal bicycles demonstrating the intersection of cutting-edge technology and consummate craftsmanship—a true marriage of art and design.

This catalogue is published in conjunction with the exhibition *Bespoke: The Handbuilt Bicycle,* on display at the Museum in the MADProjects Gallery from May 13 to August 15, 2010. This view into the world of handbuilt bicycles is presented as part of MADProjects, an ongoing program of exhibitions, guest-curated by leading voices in the field of design.

Michael Maharam, entrepreneur and bicycle enthusiast, and Sacha White, master bicycle builder, have collaborated to present these masterworks created by a renowned cadre of skilled makers. Through the exhibition, visitors are provided with the opportunity to appreciate bicycles on all levels as both elegant artifacts and high-performance machines.

We are delighted to introduce our visitors to another layer of contemporary design creativity in *Bespoke: The Handbuilt Bicycle.* Many thanks to Michael Maharam for sharing his passion and to Julie Lasky for authoring this publication, which we hope will interest cyclists worldwide.

The bicycle is one of the world's most indelible inventions. A typical example at the turn of the twentieth century had a skeletal frame of metal tubing joined in a diamond shape, and the same is true today. Indeed, if a century-old bicycle appeared on contemporary Main Street, it would attract far less attention than a car from the same era. And it would look positively fresh next to a comparably aged airplane.

Credit simplicity for this staying power. The bicycle as we know it—defined simply as a machine with two equal-size wheels that are propelled through the leg's rotational motion, which transfers energy by means of pedals to a chain or drive shaft—has been around since the 1880s. Many years and much effort had been expended to take the vehicle to that point. In the eighteenth and nineteenth centuries, several human-powered riding machines were invented and failed, and it was popularly believed that human limbs had reached their potential as instruments of mobility and that nothing could improve on the efficiency of God's design.

Once the modern bicycle overturned that conviction, there wasn't much more to do to it. Gears were added and multiplied, brakes refined, and pounds shed to produce more lightweight transport, but the effect is one of an industrial-design spa treatment rather than a total makeover. If any bicycle startles the contemporary eye, it is probably an experimental model that has tentatively traded in the diamond frame for a solid blob of carbon, or has dispensed with the traditional upright (touring) or hunched-over (racing) position in favor of a reclined seat.

No, not much is simpler than a bicycle. And not much is more complex. Bicycles are hardwired to our childhood memories but we do not retire them along with other childish things. They may be obscure, mud-caked instruments on which we rely for income, or cherished belongings as pampered as family heirlooms. They connect riders to their community and urban fabric or set them apart as rebels. They can be symbols of hidebound conformity or tokens of radical liberation.

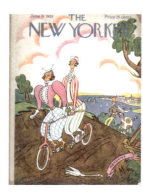

Bespoke: The Handbuilt Bicycle, an exhibition that opened at New York's Museum of Arts and Design in May 2010, to which this book serves as companion, presents these multifaceted, poetic objects in an appropriately concentrated way. Curated by Michael Maharam, a New York entrepreneur, cyclist, and bicycle collector, the show features some 20 bicycles designed in metal by six independent builders: two from America's West Coast, three from its East Coast, and one from Italy. Each bicycle presented in *Bespoke* is made by hand according to methods that have deviated little from the dawn of the craft. The range extends from racing bicycles for champion athletes to mountain and cyclocross bicycles for off-road maneuvers to city bicycles for daily commutes to elegantly stripped-down randonneur bicycles for self-supported journeys of hundreds of miles.

Despite the seeming simplicity of their forms and mechanics, bicycles offer a unique challenge to their makers. Rider and machine meet at three contact points—saddle, handlebar, and pedal. This extraordinary degree of integration, compared with that of almost any other type of sporting equipment, from bowling balls to speedboats, leaves greater risk of poor performance and discomfort if the connection between body and

bicycle isn't seamless. The custom builder's chief preoccupation is therefore with fit; simply taking a rider's measurements may require more than two hours for a single commission. Every bicycle is a highly refined piece of engineering.

Perfect fit, however, is merely one skill the builder possesses. The craft of custom bicycles also involves master metalwork: bending, welding, carving, and wrapping steel, titanium, aluminum, and carbon. A graphic artist's eye is required in the application of paint and decorative flourishes. Whereas several people may be involved in manufacturing a factory-made bicycle, the custom models exhibited in *Bespoke* are the virtuosic productions of individuals.

According to Sacha White of Vanilla Bicycles in Portland, Oregon, this constellation of skills is precisely what gives handbuilt bicycles their unique worth. White, who is a co-curator of *Bespoke* as well as a featured designer, appreciates that frame builders are riding a wave of popularity with the recent cultural renaissance of handcrafts. But he is concerned that the wave will quickly crest if the public fixates on attributes of custom bicycles that tend to receive the most attention: their fancy paint jobs, high

prices (easily $10,000–$15,000), and long wait times (five years for a Vanilla). "For interest in what we do to be lasting, we need to communicate the deeper value beyond those sound bites," White says. What must be relayed, he believes, is the builder's holistic perspective as it is translated into a unified balance of performance and art. *Bespoke* was conceived to provide such an education.

Perhaps *Bespoke*'s most important lesson is that the rigors and traditions of constructing metal bicycles leave room for a remarkable range of approaches.

In some ways, Sacha White and his fellow *Bespoke* builder Richard Sachs represent opposite ends of a spectrum. White is a renaissance designer who excels in bikes for touring, commuting, and racing. One of his most acclaimed creations is a child's tricycle with deeply affecting swooping lines. Sachs, for his part, is a monomaniac who has been building the same red-painted racing frame for three and a half decades, making incremental improvements on an object that connoisseurs long ago judged as resting at the apex.

Contrasts are also stark when one views the work of Peter Weigle, who has almost single-handedly revived the popularity of French cyclotouring, or randonneur, bicycles in America, and Jeff Jones, who builds frames for off-road riding. Weigle hand-carves the lugs that connect his bikes' tubing as if they were precious jewels, and favors green, lavender, and gold paint colors that Monet would have appreciated. Jones rejects any aspect of a bicycle that might be described as "jewelry." The only perspective that counts, he believes, is the rider's as he or she is planted in the saddle, and from that vantage point, the bike is invisible, its looks subservient to its performance. Jones's tubes are gleaming unpainted titanium or steel, and they are welded rather than lugged to accommodate his nontraditional frame designs.

Mike Flanigan and Dario Pegoretti, *Bespoke*'s remaining two builders, form another study in variance. Flanigan, a longtime resident of New England, produces sober, practical bicycles for commuting to work or carting groceries. His company, Alternative Transportation Vehicles (A.N.T.), represents bikes as something more than useful personal objects; they also contribute to a cleaner, more neighborly world. Pegoretti, a denizen

    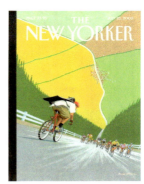

of northern Italy's hill country, makes sleek racing bicycles orna-
mented with wild paint splashes and scrawls—exotic creatures
rendered with the flair of a continental suit.

The broad strokes of such descriptions should not draw attention
away from the subtlety of each design. In his own way, Jones,
the radical, is as attentive to classic bicycle constructions as
Weigle, the conserver. Beneath the flashy surface of a Pegoretti
and the rubicund paint of a Sachs lie manifestations of
profound technical skill. Flanigan mixes elegance and whimsy
with pragmatism, and White, with his supple artistry influenced
by street and snowboarding culture, makes the demanding
balancing act of his craft look easy. It isn't.

If evidence were needed of the bicycle's dominance in twentieth-century life, it could be found on the covers of *The New Yorker* magazine. Bicycles in urban,
suburban, and rural landscapes have made cover appearances more than 100 times since the magazine was founded in 1925. Courtesy Richard Sachs

Michael Maharam is the aesthetic force behind the New York-based textile company Maharam. An avid cyclist and bicycle collector, he curated the Museum of Arts and Design exhibition *Bespoke: The Handbuilt Bicycle* with Sacha White.

Sacha White, an internationally respected frame builder, runs Vanilla Bicycles in Portland, Oregon.

Julie Lasky: What was the inspiration for *Bespoke*?

Sacha White: Michael bought a bike from me a couple of years ago. Through talking about what he wanted to do with that bike, it came out that he was acquainted with the director of the Museum of Arts and Design. Vanilla was approaching its tenth anniversary, and I thought about building ten bikes that would let me go as deep into the craft as I could, showing what we could do on a level beyond the everyday. I called him for advice, and the show morphed from that project into an exhibition about independent builders, partially as seen through my eyes—people who have inspired me in one way or another.

JL: Michael, bicycles today are made of all kinds of materials, from plastic to bamboo. What are your thoughts about limiting this exhibition's designs to metal?

Michael Maharam: I like the fact that we're doing metal for the show. It represents form being extended out into different directions. For Jeff Jones, titanium is about being novel. For Sacha, Dario Pegoretti, Richard Sachs, and, in a different sense, Peter Weigle, steel is about being traditional. And for Mike Flanigan, steel is about being utilitarian. These bikes provide a pinnacle for the market to view and from which it will derive ideas that will ultimately become commercial. If you look at our world, as we typically deal with design, unique pieces serve as inspirational sources for commercial purposes.

JL: To the untutored eye, a bicycle is a bicycle, unless it has a novelty form like some carbon-fiber frames, or it looks like Jeff's somewhat alien space frames. How do you highlight the distinctions among the traditional builders in this show?

SW: Both Dario and Richard are pushing the limits of the performance machine; Richard is working with traditional methods and joinery and tubing sizes, taking what he knows as far as construction methods and trying to perfect the form with those elements. Dario, I think, even though he comes from a place of deep tradition and history, having built 30,000 bikes for racers, has ideas of how to break out of that mold and work with manufacturers that create tubing materials, sizes, and shapes that have never been used before. Also his surface treatment is outside of the box.

MM: People aren't embellishing bikes the way Sacha does, not only in terms of his paint and graphics but also his use of uncommon materials and approaches. His bikes run across categories from pure performance—with Speedvagen—to his very elegant lavender randonneur bike. On the spectrum of traditional bike building, Sacha intersects with Richard and Dario at one end, and Peter at the other.

SW: A lot of what's created now follows market trends. The kinds of bikes Peter builds are not mainstream though they're getting more popular now.

MM: Peter's bikes reflect what most people in a place like Manhattan might aspire to own: a sophisticated alternative to the traditional black Raleigh or the heavy, utilitarian bikes that represent the Scandinavian and Dutch approach.

SW: I wouldn't associate Peter with the old Raleigh or Scandinavian setup. He's tied in with the French tradition of being a *constructeur,* looking at the bike as a whole. Instead of building frame and fork and putting components on it, he considers every little detail of the bike, and everything incorporated in the frame fits perfectly. But I agree that someone whose heartstrings are pulled by old-school British and Scandinavian upright bikes would be tugged by the old-school French bikes that Peter is doing.

MM: He's made a super commitment to a tiny niche.

JL: Where does Mike Flanigan rest in this scheme?

MM: To me, he's the court jester of it all in his own industrial utilitarian way. The deck of cards cut into the chain ring of his Truss Frame Bike is very amusing.

JL: Working on this project, I've come to appreciate the nuances and depth of the bicycle subculture, but I'm also impressed by the breadth. All of the *Bespoke* builders have international reputations. When Dario Pegoretti was diagnosed with lymphoma and getting treatment in his native Italy, fans were sending tributes from places like Memphis, Tennessee. One guy even suggested he go to Graceland.

SW: I attribute this reach to the internet. We all have these tiny hole-in-the-wall shops but if we portray ourselves accurately and effectively on the web, it can work to our advantage. I started building bike frames at the same time the web was becoming useful and practical. Before that, builders had to cultivate a following in their towns while spreading out their roots to reach a broader audience. You could only find a national following through dealers, and then builders were cutting what they made in half.

MM: When I was a teenager, the bicycles you wanted were a Schwinn Paramount or Raleigh Professional. There were not a lot of builders in those days, whereas other crafts like glass-blowing or watch-making existed broadly. It's interesting to see how explosively this world has grown.

SW: The last frame-building renaissance was in the 1970s because of the road-racing boom. You couldn't get a quality road bike from the store. It would be misaligned. Someone would go to a builder or get their hands on an Italian bike: a De Rosa or Masi.

MM: Who are your influences?

SW: Some of my heroes include Albert Eisentraut, Mark DiNucci, Jim Merz, Bruce Gordon, Tom Kellogg, Mark Nobilette. They all started from the same couple of places. Eisentraut was a big teacher.

JL: Why are handbuilt bikes having a renaissance now?

SW: In the '80s, mountain biking caught on and road biking dropped off the face of the earth. If someone wanted to stay in business they had to adapt. Through the '90s, it was a super-dry period. Richard Sachs talks about what he had to do to stay afloat during those times: building semi-production frames and selling them for $300. It was such a drastic change from where we are now. What changed it? The same thing that changed food and coffee: people are looking for something more special—

they want more of a connection to what they're using and less meaningless consumerism. They want to go smaller.

MM: I remember a little niche community that existed between San Francisco and Seattle building mountain bikes in the '80s—people like Charlie Cunningham and Gary Klein. There were bikes all around Marin which you could rent for $35 a day; or for $60, you could splurge on a custom bike built by someone like Cunningham. Sacha, you should talk about the evolution from mountain bikes to cyclocross.

SW: What happened was that mountain-biking technology went to full suspension, with suspension shocks and suspension rear ends. The independent builder or small shop that built mountain bikes couldn't compete with the R&D budgets big companies brought to the table. Their niche decreased to serving people who wanted fully rigid bikes. Cyclocross had entered the scene by a similar path as mountain bikes; for a long time the bikes weren't produced. The tradition is pretty old, from the 1950s and '60s. It's the kind of racing that happens when the road racing season ends. A cyclocross bike has a similar shape as a road bike, but clearance for fatter tires.

MM: And cantilever brakes for mud clearance.

SW: Another interesting thing about cyclocross: with major professional road racing, independent builders have been priced out of sponsoring at a major level. Someone from the Tour de France can't ride a bike branded Vanilla because Vanilla can't afford to pay $100,000. Trek probably pays millions. But because cyclocross is at a grass-roots level, someone like Richard Sachs can sponsor a winning team. In fact, many of his riders have won at a national level. Vanilla Team riders race at the national level, too. They are competing against guys sponsored by companies like Trek and Cannondale.

JL: What's happening with women in the sport?

SW: Most women in the bicycle industry would say women are being left out. The women's Tour de France doesn't get coverage. In Seattle, the payout for men is thousands; women get cooking utensils.

MM: The problem is this: it doesn't equate to bicycle sales. Women riding bicycles are generally engaging in a husband-

driven weekend hobby. I'm fascinated by the statistic that the number-one economy in the world is the U.S. economy. The second is the German economy. And the third is women in the U.S. They're largely in charge of disposable income in America. But when it comes to bicycles, women are largely non-factors. Also fundamental: for guys, bicycles are a coming-of-age ideal, a mode of establishing independence, a means to get out and get away. When you're a fourteen-year-old, that's your car. It's not the same for girls. Guys' bikes are ridden everywhere; girls' bikes sit in the garage with a flat tire.

JL: Both of you men are aesthetic perfectionists. That's what makes you so successful, and that, I would venture, is partly what's brought you together. Do you find your standards at all stressful? If you could let go of one compulsion, what would it be?

SW: I recognize that my standards take a toll on the people around me. If I didn't make a concerted effort to give positive reinforcement, the only thing that would come out of my mouth would be criticism. I try to tell my employees that it's not in my nature to sit with a finished product and soak up the good vibrations. As soon as a product is up to the level I want it to be, my mind is on to the next thing. It's the same with the business: I feel my life would be healthier if I took the time to recognize when we were experiencing a moment of success.

MM: It's a blessed and noble curse, but I don't know any other way. I fantasize about lobotomy... it's all or nothing!

JL: Sacha, I saw recently that someone sold one of your custom track bikes on eBay. How do you feel about a bespoke creation of yours finding a new life that way?

SW: It's kind of like being broken up with. My neurotic side makes me wonder, "Is it me? Did I do something wrong?" I definitely recognize that people's priorities change. I've had lots of bicycles and I've sold almost all of them. There are only one or two I'd like to keep forever. For the most part, I think it's a happy ending for all. The original owner got to experience what he got to experience and then got to pass it on.

JL: Which bike would you keep forever?

SW: Definitely the first bike I built, with Tim Paterek: a single-speed cyclocross bike. If the apocalypse were coming and I could only have one bicycle, the single-speed cyclocross would be the one: it's fast, simple, durable, and rugged enough to go off-road, but not as tank-y as a mountain bike. This one also has huge sentimental value for me. I knew literally nothing when I built it. It's simple and pretty rough, but it captures the desire I had at the time to make something that was perfect and beautiful and really complete. I didn't want to put anything on the road that was half-assed.

JL: Michael, do you have a particular bike you would never give up?

MM: It might have been my stripped-bare and battered Klein Pinnacle, which I talked Gary Klein into selling me directly in 1986. It languished for years when I came to New York, and I finally converted it into a fantastic urban cyclocross machine for my wife, Sabine, after which it was too alluring to some rotten and yet-to-be-identified thief. Hopefully somebody out there is enjoying it!

JL: Having spent some time researching the six builders in this show, I've discovered an interesting commonality: everyone, even "radicals" like Jeff Jones, seems obsessed with the bicycle designs of the past. Which aspect of cycling's history do you think is most worth preserving? Which aspects are better left behind?

MM: I'd all but dismiss the Schwinn era of the mid-'70s to mid-'80s. This was the AMC of its day, churning out mediocrity, apart from the sacred early Paramount. On the bright side, it was a sales machine and probably did a great deal to encourage Americans to take to the road—it did me, and ultimately led me to an after-school job at my local Schwinn bicycle shop. As for aspects worth preserving, I think that day has yet to come: we're in a moment of product proliferation that has brought many novel, innovative, and senseless ideas to the table, but without definition as to what will resonate with enduring character and value. One hope of this show is to influence mass producers to aspire to greater accomplishments. Hopefully, a downsized economy coupled with growing environmentalism will lead to a less material world and greater respect for thoughtful products of lasting quality… bicycles among them.

"Why should anyone steal a watch when he could steal a bicycle?" Flann O'Brien

Sacha White

Brazing the reinforcement on a dropout; carving a lug; aligning a frame; screwing on the head badge

In 1998, Sacha White was a bicycle messenger in Portland, Oregon, riding 60 to 70 miles a day, when his frame snapped. A visit to a repair shop awakened his interest in bicycle fabrication, and he enrolled in a frame-building course taught by Tim Paterek, a local artisan. Today, White's Vanilla Bicycles is known for impeccably constructed and fitted steel bikes for touring, commuting, and racing. The joints of a Vanilla are lugged or fillet-brazed with brass or silver for a smooth connection, the lugs painstakingly filed to a consistent thinness.

Born in Longmont, Colorado, near Boulder, White developed an early habit of improving bicycles. As a child, his first work of customization was to pilfer expensive Campagnolo Record components from his father's Schwinn Paramount and have them fitted piece by piece onto his much inferior Schwinn Le Tour. Through his teens, he developed a passion for restoring old Vespa and Lambretta scooters, but the interest dropped away once he moved to Portland and became connected to the local bike culture. He hasn't owned a car since 2004.

For White, the independent frame builder's value lies in a holistic approach. Such artisans must master a constellation of skills that depend on different talents. First is measuring the client for fit, taking into account a range of motions and postures. Next is mapping out the bicycle's geometry—calculating the angles, laying out the wheels—to produce a certain ride quality, from laid-back to hyper-responsive. Then comes the translation of schematic drawings into metal, a feat of engineering. "This is really where the craft takes place," White says. "It's where skill and precision are so important, and where a proven method of steps 1 to 100 done properly will yield a straight, structurally sound frame." Finally, builders "must be able to incorporate their own style and artistic design touches so that the client gets something unique and beautiful."

Even among builders, White is notable for his range of services. He custom-designs components such as featherweight fender mounts for lights, stainless-steel chain guards that prevent pants legs from getting soiled, and water bottles with hardwood caps that evoke vintage French cycling accessories. Three years ago, he opened Coat, an in-house paint shop, to guarantee efficient, high-quality paint jobs for all Vanilla bicycles. The shop also services a handful of other independent builders.

White's preference for steel as a building material is anything but quaint, or even traditional. "The levels have been pushed with steel," he says. "It can be as high-tech as anything else. You can build frames in the 2.5- to 3-pound range that are darn near as light as titanium or carbon."

A former competitive cyclist and current cyclocross team sponsor, White recently launched Speedvagen, a brand of small-batch production racing frames that are available in a wider range of materials, including carbon fiber. The bikes are built collaboratively with other respected builders. Dario Pegoretti participated in designing the Speedvagen Track Machine, to be produced in the summer of 2010. "I am still scratching the surface of what it is to make bikes," White says. "There is a lifetime of learning in this."

Vanilla Track Bicycle

Built to be raced in a velodrome, this bicycle incorporates signature Vanilla details: subtle unexpected color combinations; stainless top-tube protectors (handy in the event of a crash); a one-piece bar-stem combo built from segments of machined and hand-carved chromoly steel; handmade titanium seat post; and carved stainless lugs.

Handmade titanium-lugged seat post

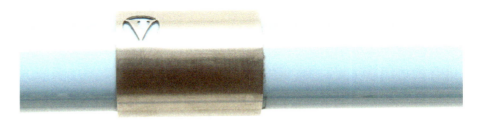

Top-tube protector, a feature of Vanilla track bikes

Vanilla's distinctive bar/stem combo

Hand-carved lugs in stainless steel

Vintage Campagnolo hub

Chrome on drive-side chain stay protects tube from wear

Vanilla Randonneur Bicycle

Light and fast, this model features subtle geometrical innovations that make it easy to maneuver in long road races. Details include carved and thinned lugs, with shorelines that are consistent throughout the bike. The paint is a fine-grain metallic that accentuates the lug lines with a subtle glow and sharp shadows. The bottle cage, bottle, and hardwood cap were made in-house, as was the leather chain-stay protector.

Classic Vanilla details: precisely fitted fender lines, stainless-steel "V" dropouts, and leather chain-stay protecto

Kid's Utility Bicycle

In its smallest iteration, this bicycle fits a six-year-old, but its saddle height, stem length, crank length, and handlebars can be adjusted to accommodate children up to twelve. Large wheels evoke the style of old roadsters and help the bike to look proportional as the owner grows.

A classic Brooks saddle enhances the bike's vintage look. Front and rear lighting system is powered by a generator built into the front hub.

Speedvagen Track Machine

White's Speedvagen brand produces bicycles in runs of 30 to 40 frames that share the same design elements (tubing, dropouts, joinery, color palette). This track-racing prototype features hollow "tubular truss" dropouts and a top tube reinforced with built-in thickness rather than with an external metal protector. The Speedvagen name is cut of out of the steel head tube, revealing the carbon fiber reinforcement inside. The first run will be produced this summer with Dario Pegoretti as guest builder.

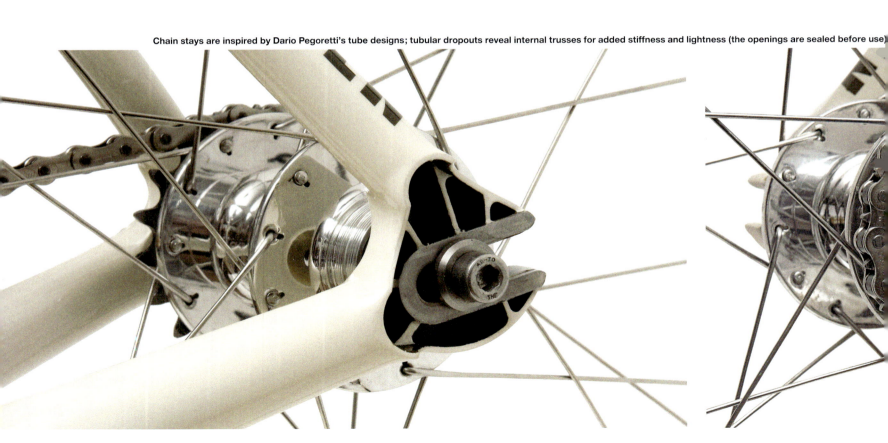

Chain stays are inspired by Dario Pegoretti's tube designs; tubular dropouts reveal internal trusses for added stiffness and lightness (the openings are sealed before use).

This bike features a custom-designed seat tube with integrated seat mast. The head tube is reinforced with a carbon fiber sleeve.

Tricycle

White designed this tricycle for his daughter Delilah in a series of napkin sketches.
The stainless-steel frame is made from several segments that have been welded together
and sanded to give the appearance of a single piece. The elliptical-shaped grips of cherry wood
and polished aluminum are inspired by bicycles from the turn of the twentieth century.

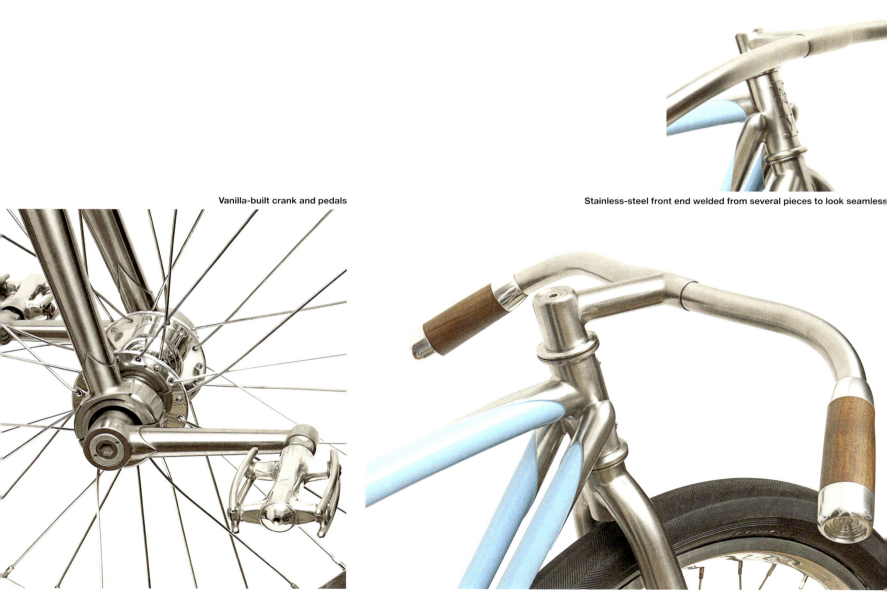

Vanilla-built crank and pedals

Stainless-steel front end welded from several pieces to look seamless

Canted rear wheels inspired by hot rods

Jeff Jones

Tack welding a fork; burnishing a titanium frame; view of shop; working at the mill

A pioneering designer of mountain bikes, Jeff Jones rejects the use of suspension to cushion a ride over rough terrain. Instead, he builds rigid frames with unique titanium or steel geometries, which, combined with optional 29-inch wheels and fat tires, absorb much of the shock, allowing cyclists to feel connected to but not jolted by the earth. Jones allows the look of a bike to unfold naturally from his demands for comfort and control. The results are designs both championed for their beauty and challenged for their oddity. But Jones only cares about appearance from the rider's point of view, when the bicycle disappears and all that remains visible is the road or trail.

Raised in Southern California, Jones built his first bikes as a child. He chopped up and reassembled frames his mother brought home from garage sales and rode the bikes over punishing courses in imitation of his hero Evel Knievel. He perfected his craft in the workshop of Gary Turner, whose Santa Ana California-based GT Bicycles produced early BMX models. Jones left GT after six years to open his own bike shops. In 2002, he began his frame-building business, which he runs with his wife, Sheila, in the Oregon woods. His evolving designs for space and diamond frames are produced in small production runs, and he turns out roughly ten custom bicycles each year.

After studying bridges, cranes, and airplane wings, Jones concluded that most structures are designed to be more rigid in one direction than the other on a two-dimensional plane. A Jones frame is distinguished by lateral stiffness combined with vertical flexibility. Its geometry ensures that the rider assumes a comfortable position, with the legs acting as natural shock absorbers. Four tubes are welded to the head tub for stability; the fork is stiffened with a truss; and the seat tube is braced low, which allows it to flex back and take in jolts that would normally be transmitted to the saddle. Jones's H-shape handlebars allow riders to shift weight forward for climbing or for aerodynamic positions, or to lean back for downhill runs.

"My customers say they are more at one with the bike; they can feel the trail," Jones says. "It's like driving a Porsche, where you feel you're in control and that you and the machine are a single unit. I believe that without suspension, riding is so much more efficient and lighter and smoother, and you become a better rider."

Though Jones creates bikes to negotiate rocks, ruts, bumps, logs, tight turns, and trails many cyclists might consider unrideable, he is reluctant to assign them the usual rubrics of mountain, cross-country, road, or downhill. "I want my bikes to ride anywhere," he says. "It's a tool for people to move."

Jones Bike

Jones's unique titanium SpaceFrame with truss fork is built to be both rigid and compliant, absorbing shocks while ensuring control over rocky trails and tight turns. It accommodates large wheels and provides clearance for mud and gravel. With a change of tires, it is equally effective for road riding. The H-shape handlebars support a wide variety of hand positions.

Truss fork detail

Head badge; drive train featuring six gears rather than the usual nine for a stronger chain line

Jones Small Bike

Jones custom-built this traditional titanium diamond frame with truss fork for his daughter, Marley. The handlebar is his Cut H-bar design

Cranks and pedals adapted for child rider

Wide front hub unique to Jones bikes

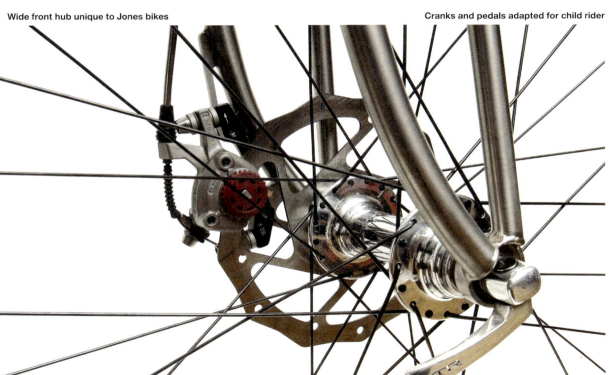

Jones's Cut H-Bar handlebars

Dario Pegoretti

Pegoretti in studio kitchen; wheel display; studio paint shop

Dario Pegoretti has produced an estimated 30,000 bicycles in steel and aluminum in his 35-year career, a substantial number of which have been ridden by international cycling stars, including Miguel Indurain, Marco Pantani, and Floyd Landis. After setting aside an early ambition to become a teacher, he apprenticed in the Veronese factory of his father-in-law, the legendary Italian frame builder Luigino Milani. Today, Pegoretti works with a handful of assistants in Caldonazzo, a small mountain town in northern Italy. His quaint, disheveled workshop, where eclectic music bursts from homemade speakers and amplifiers, belies his rigorously refined designs and technical innovations: Pegoretti was a European pioneer in the now common practice of TIG-welding to produce lugless bicycle frames, and he has worked closely with manufacturers to develop specialized tubing. Where his eccentric personality finds an outlet is in the hand-painted graphic patterns that ornament many of his road and track bikes, and in the model names, which are often inspired by jazz and popular music compositions.

Big Leg Emma, for example, a steel bicycle with custom-designed large-diameter tubes, some featuring horizontal struts inside for lateral rigidity, is named after a song from Frank Zappa's 1967 album *Absolutely Free.* This bicycle has been described as "an effective, efficient pedaling platform for a large or very aggressive racer."

Responsorium, a supple stainless-steel bicycle for which tubing is also fabricated exclusively for Pegoretti (in runs so limited that the bike has a two-year waiting list), is named after an album by the Argentine musician Dino Saluzzi. Responsorium is available in a choice of two paint schemes: Catch the Spider, a pattern of apple green rectangles on a metallic blue field, and Ciavete, a gestural design based solely on Pegoretti's whim the day he is painting it.

In March 2007, Pegoretti was diagnosed with lymphoma. His many supporters were moved to find him posting a website apology for the slowdown in production while he received treatment. The website Competitive Cyclist invited fans to send supportive words and bike photos to its "Note to Dario" section. Twenty-two pages of goodwill ensued:

Dario, Crashed my new Marcelo on a group ride the day your condition was announced. I thought I saw a teardrop seep from the small chip in the paint... as I cried, so did the world. Get well soon. Jeff

Jeff, Tuscaloosa, AL

Big Leg Emma, glistening orange. Pacific Coast Highway. Swirling wind. Sun glints, bounces off sweat raining down. Glance at the coolest chain stays this side of heaven and chunk that sucker big ring small cog. Tires humming. Legs pounding. Flash of silver and yellow off the top tube. Asphalt rolling. The bike is my body is the road is the bike. Climbing now. Fighting for air. Upwards on wings of silken pain. Suddenly, far far below, ocean and mist. Sun overhead now, burning through clothing. Descending. Swervy steel humming sweetness. The sound of endless childhood flying on rails of joy... Get well soon, Dario. Emma needs a friend made to her exact likeness in stainless, painted with love from Italy.

Matt Johnson, Los Angeles, CA

In February 2008 Pegoretti was named Frame Builder of the Year at the North American Handmade Bicycle Show in Portland, Oregon. Upon receiving the award, he said, "It is an extreme honor to be recognized in this way. It is my hope that the frames I make are used on the roads and not hung as art on the wall." He is now back to hand-building 300 frames each year, including a recent collaboration on a cyclocross design with Sacha White's racing bicycle brand, Speedvagen.

Love #3

This aluminum road bike, when fitted with a carbon fiber fork, weighs as little as 2.5 pounds. It takes its name from a song by the Charles Lloyd Quartet as well as from the unidentified "third love" of Pegoretti's life. The barbed-wire surface design is called Guantánamo

Pegoretti designs all of his own tubing for specific models. Dropouts (below right and opposite) are enlarged to fit oversize chain stays

Day Is Done

Named after a Nick Drake song as covered by the jazz pianist Brad Mehldau, Day Is Done
is a recent addition to Pegoretti's repertory of steel framesets. This example features a
Venetian Stucco paint scheme, intended to recall the rough, warm-colored finishes of Venice's
buildings

Pegoretti's subtle application of paint can distract the eye from a frame's technical refinements

Responsorium

An album by the Argentine musician Dino Saluzzi inspired the name of this stainless-steel bicycle. Pegoretti takes a full day to apply the Ciavete design, which is whatever he feels like painting that day; no two are alike. Early examples were influenced by the artists Emilio Vedova and Jean-Michel Basquiat

Aligning forks; putting a knife-edge detail on a dropout; turning a crown race on a lathe; riding in the Connecticut countryside

Peter Weigle

Originally produced in France, randonneur and sportif bicycles are lightweight models outfitted for long-distance rides. They attracted little interest in the U.S. until Peter Weigle, drawn to their elegance and practicality, began creating his own interpretations. Now he and other builders who have followed his lead serve a growing number of enthusiasts.

Weigle grew up on a dairy farm in the Berkshire Mountains of Massachusetts. An avid skier, he worked in ski retail and refinishing shops until a chance meeting with a representative of Witcomb USA led to an invitation to travel to London in 1973 for a seven-months' apprenticeship at Witcomb Lightweight Cycles. It was there that he met Richard Sachs, who had arrived at Witcomb the month before. Upon his return, Weigle worked at Witcomb USA until 1977, when its owner closed it. "I thought I would do something else," Weigle recalls, "but a week later, I bought all the equipment and set up my own shop in East Haddam, Connecticut." JP Weigle Cycles is currently located in the nearby town of Lyme.

Thoughout his career, Weigle has anticipated and helped to foster the bicycle market's shifting enthusiasms. An accomplished athlete with numerous wins, including Connecticut state road and time-trial championships and a national cyclocross championship, he proved his racing frames were competitive and built similar ones for a growing number of admiring customers.

In 1982, just as mountain bikes were first becoming popular in the American West but before they had been seen in the East, a friend in California sent Weigle several photographs and a rough drawing of a custom-made mountain bike he had recently acquired. Weigle built a similar bike and became an ardent proponent and serious mountain-bike racer. Again, his customers followed his example and bought his bikes.

Ten years later when the simple mountain bike became complicated with suspension systems that could be outdated overnight, and the once cult-like races became "festivals," Weigle went back to his roots and produced mostly high-end racing bikes again.

Then, at the turn of the millennium, Weigle fell in love once more. This time the object of his affections was the French cyclo-touring, or randonneur, bicycle. The classic design inspired him to produce his own version, and he has been building randonneur bikes ever since. Designed for speed and comfort over long distances, these bicycles feature wide tires with low rolling resistance for comfort, and fenders to help the rider stay dry if it rains. The bikes may be equipped with lighting systems and a traditional handlebar bag mounted on the front rack for food, clothing, and extra gear. Many of Weigle's randonneur bikes are used for extended day rides, and some are entered in cyclotouring events, including qualifiers for Paris–Brest–Paris, a 750-mile race with a 90-hour time limit.

Weigle's detail work is legendary: he hand-cuts many of his own lugs, whose curves evoke the florid lines of French examples from the 1950s and 1960s. "I don't make reproductions or ritualistic reenactments of things from that period," he says. "I try to honor the emotional and visual spirit of those bikes and add my own design elements and style. Every line and shape is important to me and I want my eyes to smile when I look at one of my bikes."

Green Randonneur Bicycle

Weigle chose flowing lug lines and a soft French green color to highlight his customer's blend of polished vintage and modern parts. The custom-made front rack features a removable decaleur for a handlebar bag and attachment points for a powerful LED flashlight. This bike was judged Best Randonneur at Le Cirque du Cyclisme, 2009.

Custom details include French-inspired lugs, frame-fitted pump, and taillight.

Ladies' Randonneur Bicycle

This frame was inspired by bicycles built by René Herse of France in the 1950s and 1960s. Such bikes had rakish lines and were expected to perform as well as the traditional diamond frames of their day, in part because of the secondary lateral stays that added triangulation and rigidity to the structure. Vintage components complement the traditional frame construction.

Vintage Simplex rear derailleur

Brazed-on MAFAC center pulls

Custom front rack, handmade light

Vintage Idéale saddle

Gold Sportif Bicycle

A racing bicyclist with a collection of vintage parts commissioned this fendered "hot rod" with traditional lines. Weigle embellished a set of classic Nervex "Super Legere" lugs with extra points, and custom cut the needle-point fork crown. The frame features delicate curved bridges and minimalist rear dropouts. The Spartan gold finish highlights the lug work. This bike won Best in Show at Le Cirque du Cyclisme, 2009.

Embellished Nervex "Super Legere" lugs with blue highlights

Custom-drilled Campagnolo Nuovo Tipo hubs with added wing nuts

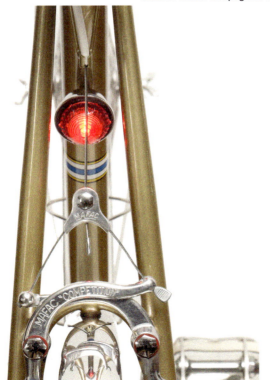

Aligning a frame; powder coating; doing a wheel check

Mike Flanigan

Some bicycles are like thoroughbred racehorses: sensitive, high-performance machines straining for speed. Others are workhorses: solid, upright conveyances for people and cargo. Mike Flanigan, a frame builder since 1983, founded Alternative Needs Transportation (A.N.T.) in 2001 to fill a perceived void in America's utility bicycle stable. A.N.T. bikes are equipped with baskets, racks, bells, lights, kickstands, fenders, chain guards, and easy-to-maintain internal gear and braking systems— practical features for the urban cyclist. And while these handmade creations may lack obvious dazzle, they are highly refined machines, with inspirations from vintage models and numerous subtle flourishes. More than mere artifacts, A.N.T. bikes support a culture of cycling that Flanigan considers vital for physical, environmental, and societal health. "I am part of the locavore movement," he declares. "My business is part of the community, and my bikes are part of the community."

Frame builders often tinker with higher orders of technology— hot rods, motorcycles, or scooters, say—before devoting themselves to the bicycle's simple mechanics. Flanigan, who was raised in Texas, is the rare builder who began working in a defense factory that produced F-16 fighter jets while he also managed a bike shop. At the time, he was in his early twenties. Seeing only a destiny of toil among 26,000 fellow drudges, he schemed to escape. If factories were in his future, he preferred those that made bicycles.

He talked his way into a job at Fat City Cycles in Boston, where he learned to excel at TIG welding and painting. ("Finish work is hard," he has recounted. "It has to look perfect; you're at the end of the line and you have to make up lost time for the rest of the shop.") When Fat City was sold in 1994, Flanigan and a half-dozen colleagues launched an employee-owned company, Independent Fabrication (IF), the noted producer of custom, though factory-built, bicycles.

Propelled by the emotional struggle of running a business with several strong-willed partners, and by his growing interest in utility bikes, Flanigan went off on his own in 2001. An environ- mentalist sensibility nurtured since childhood led him to envision the many ways properly designed bicycles could contribute to the health of communities as well as individuals. Inspired by a photo showing the celebrated French builder René Herse with a touring bike fitted with a front platform rack, he built his first fixed-gear Light Roadster with D-Rack and tested it on a cross-country trip to Seattle.

The Light Roadster became the signature product in the early days of A.N.T. It was joined by Flanigan's Basket Bike, which features a frame-mounted wire basket that can hold up to four bags of groceries, and a small, 20-inch front wheel effortlessly supporting the load. Another A.N.T. specialty is classic frame designs inspired by the turn of the twentieth century, with top tubes supported by curved trusses, swept-back handle-bars, and chain rings into which have been carved abstract patterns of playing-card suits.

Although black is his preferred paint color, Flanigan offers a spectrum of 188 powder-coat hues. And though he refuses to put lettering or other insignia on his bikes, the acid-etched brass A.N.T. logo attached to every head tube makes a powerful statement about the unique, if unshowy, value of his creations.

Truss Frame Bike

A bridge truss welded to the top tube echoes bike designs from the turn of the twentieth century. Like the Basket Bike, this steel bicycle features whimsical A.N.T. details such as a chain ring with hollowed out playing-card suits and an acid-etched brass A.N.T. nameplate—the only insignia Flanigan will allow on his frames

Rear dropout with screws for chain adjustment; turned-brass valve cap adapted from hardware-store lampshade top

Full suit chain rin

Early-20th-century-style bridge truss

Basket Bike

Inspired by vintage French postal delivery bicycles, this steel bike is designed to distribute weight to the frame rather than the wheels. A small front wheel aids in maneuverability under heavy loads

Enclosed chain case

Handmade Parisian-style handlebars

Handmade frame-mounted basket

A.N.T. insignia carved out of pedal

Brazing in workshop; pile of handlebar pieces; new studio in transition, winning 2009 Granogue cyclocross race

Richard Sachs

Throughout more than three decades as a builder, Richard Sachs has primarily made one kind of bicycle (for racing) in one kind of material (steel) painted in one color (red). And yet he sees nothing repetitive in this approach. An idealist who sets out to create the perfect bicycle with every attempt (and has come close fewer than ten times out of thousands, he estimates), Sachs insists that the tasks of designing, cutting, brazing, and coaxing the material are so organic, and often so confounding, that he is unable to make the same frame twice. Not only is each Sachs frame as variable as the person it's fitted for, it also reflects its maker's mood as he tends to the dozens of different processes required to produce and assemble it. Even the metal offers up varied characteristics, he says, depending on the batch. In reaching for impossible standards, however, Sachs continuously refines his tools and processes. The results are machines of uniform excellence that are prized throughout the world.

Sachs claims that serendipity brought him to his business, but his history suggests a compulsion to build bicycles from the start. "To be sure," he later wrote, "the bicycle was the tool, but the arena of competition and its history would become a passion. Others may have had a technical interest to dabble in human powered vehicles or alternative forms of transportation. Some may have had inclinations to pursue a craftsman's life and found their way as frame builders. I just wanted to make bicycles like the revered European builders who were supplying the roadmen of the world, and whose names were on the down-tubes next to me in my earliest days in the peloton."

Raised in suburban New Jersey, Sachs first developed his relentless interest in performance when he competed in bicycle races in his teens. When his admission to Goddard College was delayed for a semester, he boarded a bus from New York to Burlington, Vermont, to present himself for a bike mechanic's job that he had seen advertised in *The Village Voice*. On finding the job filled, he embarked on an extensive letter-writing campaign to offer his services for free to any shop that would train him in frame-building.

It was thus that Sachs made his way in 1972 to Witcomb Lightweight Cycles, a family business in South London, England, that also provided early tutelage to Peter Weigle. Sachs stayed almost a year, until his money ran out. Upon returning, he and Weigle worked briefly at an American branch of Witcomb that was launched to meet the growing demand for high-performance bicycles, encouraged by the 1970s fitness movement. In 1975, Sachs opened his own shop in Chester, Connecticut. Recently, he moved to Warwick, Massachusetts.

Through 35 years of seeking to build the elusive perfect frame, Sachs has also tested the performance of his bicycles as both a racer who has qualified to ride in the USA Cycling National Championships six times on the road and twice on the track, and as the sponsor since 1992 of one of America's most successful cyclocross teams.

"All the new materials, tube shapes, or joining processes available to the industry cannot mask the compromises that are endemic to mass-produced or even low-volume frame-building," he has stated. "Little, if anything at all, can cover up the shortcuts taken by other manufacturers whose main goal is to produce the most units at the lowest cost. The bike industry makes money. I make bikes."

Track Racing Bicycle

Sachs makes few bicycles for racing in the velodrome. This unique example pays homage to traditional craft with a frame constructed from tubing, lugs, and steel from the 1970s. The components are contemporary.

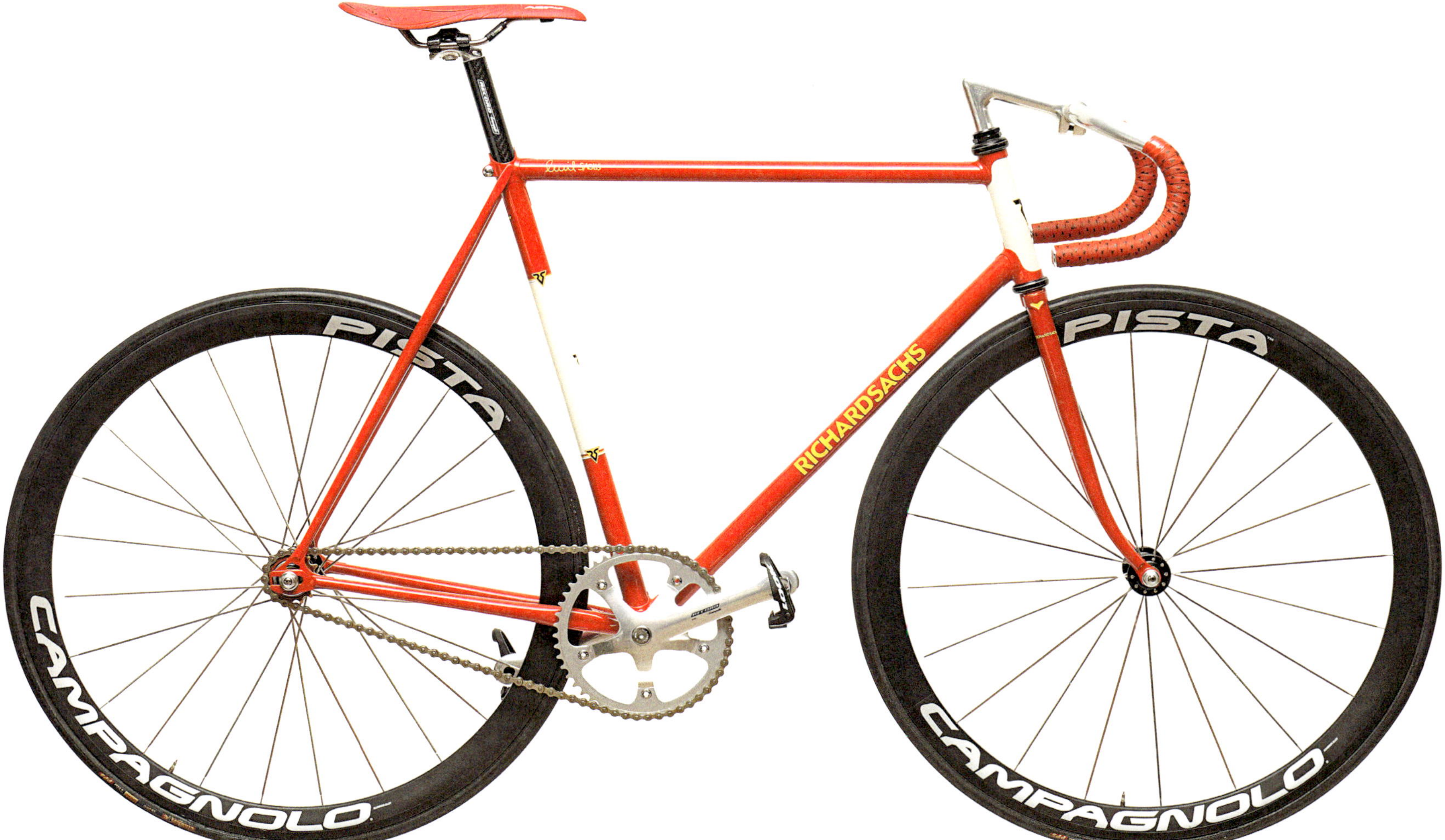

PISTA
PISTA
RICHARDSACHS
CAMPAGNOLO
CAMPAGNOLO

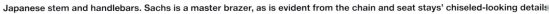

Japanese stem and handlebars. Sachs is a master brazer, as is evident from the chain and seat stays' chiseled-looking details

Road Racing Bicycle

**Sachs conceived his Signature frame in 1978 when he decided to concentrate all o
his efforts on building superior bicycles for which construction time and cost were of mino
or secondary consideration. The tubing and lugs were designed in-house and made
exclusively for Richard Sachs Cycles**

Sachs designs his own lugs, fork crowns, and dropouts and distributes them to other bike makers. His head badge is a stylized "RS.

Team Cyclocross Racing Bike

An example of the bicycles raced by the Richard Sachs–RGM Watches cyclocross team; it is assembled with components supplied by the team's industry sponsors: Cole, Oval Concepts, Cane Creek, Clement, Crank Brothers, Sram, and Wippermann. These bicycles have won 10 U.S. National Championships since 1997

Sachs makes eight to twelve of these bicycles each year, only for members of his cyclocross team. The bikes usually last no more than two seasons

Cyclocross Racing Bike

This is one of a matching pair of Sachs's own bicycles from his 2009 cyclocross campaign. In that season, Sachs raced 23 times, won six events, and finished as the highest ranked rider of nearly 1,400 participants in the USA Cycling Masters (30 years+) category.

The mud on this bicycle was preserved from the USA National Cyclocross Championship in Bend, Oregon, Sachs's last race in 2009

"When I see an adult on a bicycle, I do not despair for the future of the human race." H.G. Wells

Sacha White
Berto, Frank J. *The Dancing Chain: History and Development of the Derailleur Bicycle*, 3rd ed. San Francisco: Cycle Publishing/Van der Plas, 2009.
Bouvet, Philippe, et al. *Paris-Roublaix: A Journey Through Hell.* Boulder, CO: VeloPress, 2007.
Byrne, David. *Bicycle Diaries.* New York: Viking, 2009.
Elliott, Christine, and David Jablonka. *Custom Bicycles: A Passionate Pursuit.* Mulgrave, Victoria: Images Publishing, 2009.
Hurst, Robert. *The Cyclist's Manifesto: The Case for Riding on Two Wheels Instead of Four.* Guilford, CT: FalconGuides, 2009.

Jeff Jones
McGurn, James. *On Your Bicycle: An Illustrated History of Cycling.* New York: Facts on File, 1987.
Perry, David B. *Bike Cult: The Ultimate Guide to Human-Powered Vehicles.* New York: Four Walls Eight Windows, 1995.
Sharp, Archibald. *Bicycles and Tricycles: A Classic Treatise on Their Design and Production.* New York: Dover Publications, 2003.
Smith, Robert A. *A Social History of the Bicycle.* New York: American Heritage Press, 1972.
Wilson, David Gordon. *Bicycling Science,* 3rd ed. Cambridge, MA: The MIT Press, 2004.

Dario Pegoretti
Federazione Ciclistica Italiana [Italian Cycling Federation].
Ciclismo [Cycling magazine].
Fiz, Alberto, ed. *L'Arte della bicicletta da Duchamp a Rauschenberg* [The Art of the Bicycle from Duchamp to Rauschenberg]. Milan: De Agostini Rizzoli, 2001.
Mura, Gianni. *Giallo sul giallo* [Yellow on Yellow]. Milan: Feltrinelli, 2007.
Rouleur Photography Annual. Vol. 1. London: Rapha Racing Ltd., 2007.
Wilson, David Gordon. *Bicycling Science,* 3rd ed. Cambridge, MA.: The MIT Press, 2004.

Peter Weigle
Heine, Jan. *The Golden Age of Handbuilt Bicycles: Craftsmanship, Elegance and Function.* New York: Rizzoli/Seattle: Vintage Bicycle Press, 2010.
Noguchi-san and Fumiyo Noguchi. *100 Years of Bicycle Component and Accessory Design: Authentic Reprint Edition of The Data Book.* San Francisco: Van der Plas Publications, 1998.
New Cycling magazine (Japan). "René Herse." Vol. 39, No. 450, 2001.
Rebour, Daniel. *Cycles de Competition et Randonneuses.* Paris: Technique & Vulgarisation, 1976.
Rebour, Daniel. *La Pratique du Vélo.* Paris: Technique & Vulgarisation, 1949.

Photo credits

Mike Flanigan
Oliver, Tony. *Touring Bikes: A Practical Guide.* Marlborough, U.K.:
Crowood Press, 1990.
Pridmore, Jay, and Jim Hurd. *The American Bicycle.* Osceola, WI:
Motorbooks International, 2000.
Savage, Barbara. *Miles from Nowhere: A Round the World Bicycle Adventure.*
Seattle: Mountaineers Books, 1983.
Various. *Encycleopedia: The International Buyer's Guide to Alternatives in Cycling.*
New York: Overlook TP, 1993–2001.
Wilhelm, Tim, and Glenda Wilhelm. *Bicycle Touring Book: The Complete Guide
to Bicycle Recreation.* Emmaus, PA: Rodale Press, 1980.

Richard Sachs
Beaumont, Richard. *Purdey's: The Guns and the Family.* Devon, U.K.:
David & Charles, 1984.
Kazuyuki, Takahashi. *Les Créateurs du Temps*. Tokyo: Shellman Co. Ltd., 2004.
Marchese, John. *The Violin Maker: Finding a Centuries-Old Tradition in a Brooklyn
Workshop.* New York: Harper Perennial, 2007.
Nakashima, George. *The Soul of a Tree: A Woodworker's Reflections.*
Tokyo: Kodansha International, 1988.
St. John, Allen. *Clapton's Guitar: Watching Wayne Henderson Build the Perfect
Instrument.* New York: Free Press, 2006.
Schmidt, Paul. *Acquired of the Angels: The Lives and Works of Master Guitar
Makers John D'Angelico and James L. D'Aquisto.* 2nd Ed. Lanham, MD:
The Scarecrow Press, 1998.

Published on the occasion of the exhibition
Bespoke: The Handbuilt Bicycle
at the Museum of Arts and Design, New York
May 13–August 15, 2010

Bespoke: The Handbuilt Bicycle is made possible by the generous support of

maharam

Julie Lasky
Bespoke: The Handbuilt Bicycle

Concept: Julie Lasky
Contributors: Michael Maharam, Sacha White, D. James Dee (photographs)

Design: Integral Lars Müller / Lars Müller, Res Eichenberger
Proofreading: Rita Forbes
Production: Amelie Solbrig
Lithography: Lithotronic Media GmbH, Dreieich, Germany
Printing and Binding: Kösel, Altusried-Krugzell, Germany

Lars Müller Publishers
Baden, Switzerland
www.lars-muller-publishers.com

ISBN 978-3-03778-204-0

Printed in Germany

9 8 7 6 5 4 3 2